CLAIRE WINTLE - LONDON COLLEGE OF DANCE & DRAMA
1981

Technique
for the
Ballet Arti

GW00649979

OLGA SPESSIVTZEVA

Technique
for the
Ballet Artiste

FREDERICK MULLER LIMITED
LONDON

First published in Great Britain 1967
by Frederick Muller Ltd.
London NW2 6LE

Copyright © 1967 Anton Dolin

New Impression 1978

All rights reserved. No part of this publication may be
reproduced, stored in a retrieval system, or transmitted, in
any form or by any means, electronic, mechanical, photo-
copying, recording or otherwise, without the prior permission
of Frederick Muller Limited.

ISBN 0 584 10297 6

British Library Cataloguing in Publication Data

Spessivtzeva, Olga
Technique for the ballet artiste.
1. Ballet
I. Title
792.8'2   GV1788

ISBN 0-584-10297-6

Printed in Great Britain by
Biddles Ltd, Guildford, Surrey

Dedicated to
THE COUNTESS ALEXANDRA TOLSTOY
May 1963

Introduction

by Anton Dolin

Olga Spessivtzeva was, in my opinion, the greatest classical ballerina of the twentieth century. The nobility, the purity of her poise and line, the breath-taking perfection of her technique were equalled by no one. As a very young member of the *corps de ballet* I saw her rehearse for two months. Then, for a further three months, either on stage or watching from the wings of the Alhambra Theatre, I never missed a step she danced. That was in 1921–22 and the ballet was Serge Diaghilev's production of *The Sleeping Beauty*. I can still see Olga Spessivtzeva dancing the lovely solo of Princess Aurora in Act II. Those magnificent arabesques and attitudes at the beginning of the variation, the slow, perfectly executed series of two unsupported pirouettes, from an open fourth, turning with her slender, long two arms in fifth position (above her head) and finishing as she began in an open fourth, her right arm stretched well forward, her left in perfect line at the back.

The vision scene of Act III she was indeed a phantom. Then in the last act she again was the radiant Princess Aurora with her legs of steel and her wonderful, perfectly arched insteps over her feet that were encased in point shoes. With her partner, Pierre Vladimirov as Prince Charming, Olga Spessivtzeva was the first to execute in the grand adagio what is now known and accepted as the "fish dive", two *en dedans* pirouettes, being caught almost with her head touching the floor, her two legs parallel with her partner's shoulder and held by him with the left hand and arm, the right one free. Comparisons are odious. Today's generation who, alas, never saw Olga Spessivtzeva dance, can think and remember Margot Fonteyn. I saw the latter dance in 1948

The Sleeping Beauty at the Royal Opera House. There were moments, no, much more than moments, when I thought I was looking at Olga Spessivtzeva. In my opinion, only Margot Fonteyn of the present day's great ballerinas matched the perfection and artistry of Olga Spessivtzeva in 1921. In 1932 I had the honour of dancing with Olga Spessivtzeva at the Savoy Theatre. I was her "Albrecht", she was my "Giselle".

I saw her dance. I danced with her. As critics said, "it was the greatest exhibition of purely classical dancing that has been seen in London." Effortless and ethereal, she was the shy, lighthearted peasant girl of Act I, the "Wili" of Act II. In my opinion, only three other great ballerinas approached her rendering of this balletic and acting master-piece of the Romantic Ballet. Galina Ulanova when we first saw her dance in London in 1959 with the Bolshoi Ballet in Act I, Yvette Chauviré and Alicia Markova's wonderful dancing in *Giselle*. I re-member talking with Galina Ulanova at a reception which Dame Margot Fonteyn and her husband, Dr. Arias, gave for the company at their home, the Panamanian Embassy. Speaking and understanding Russian, I was placed at the table with the great dancer who had danced that evening "Giselle". "Dolin, you danced with Olga Spessivtzeva. Tell me, how is my interpretation and hers?" "Madam, seeing you dance in Act I was as if I was on stage myself and watching Olga. Your quick, shy looks, your playing and your spontaneous dancing was so like her." Alas, we had little time to talk for we were soon inter-rupted by someone who did not seem anxious for any further conver-sation in Russian. Those were the early days of the "Russian invasion" and it was not easy, as it is now, to converse at length without suspicion, with the Russian artistes. I have given these four comparisons to enable the reader to form, I hope, some clearer idea of what the dancing of Olga Spessivtzeva was like, especially in these two ballets which were her greatest roles. Except for a few appearances in Australia and in South America at the Colon Opera, Olga Spessivtzeva retired from dancing with a farewell performance at the Paris Opera Comique in 1935, dancing the role of Odette in *Swan Lake*, Act IV, I never saw her dance the dual role of Odile.

She was in New York in 1939. At the end of 1940 her health broke down. Tragically and seriously so.

For twenty-two years she was lost to the dance. Then, as I have written in her biography *The Sleeping Ballerina*, she awoke and began to take her place once again in normal life. Free, and away from the mental home where she had spent nearly a quarter of a century, she began again to take an interest in the Ballet. Living happily at the Tolstoy Foundation, Nyack, New York, she has her photos, books, and writes incessantly. She has her Russian friends to talk to. Her older ones can visit her in peace, none more faithful than Felia Dubrovska and her husband Pierre Vladimirov, who live and teach in New York at the School of American Ballet. She visits the ballet and though, as she says, "many changes", nevertheless she enjoys herself and expresses her opinions in no uncertain terms.

Recently she saw a performance of *Giselle*. As she said to me, "This is the first time, Anton, I have ever seen *Giselle* from the public." Actually she had seen a performance of Act II in 1940 at the New York Lewisham Stadium when Nana Gollner and I danced. But those were the beginning of clouded days. This last occasion she witnessed Ruth Ann Koesun and John Gilpin dancing with the American Ballet Theatre Company for their 25th anniversary season (1965) at the Lincoln State Theatre. Together with the Director, Miss Lucia Chase, I sat with Olga. She loved the performance and afterwards went back stage to meet the two principal artistes. To them, in Russian, she said, "You danced with great purity. Very, very good."

At this time Olga Spessivtzeva gave me the manuscript of this book which she calls *Technique for the Ballet Artiste*. Two years ago she asked me to try and find a series of similar exercises she had written about 1932. During the Second World War her studio home and her effects had been sold in Paris. Olga was in America, forgotten except by a few. The Germans had occupied Paris and nothing could be done to save her possessions. Though both Serge Lifar in Paris and I in New York tried our best to prevent it. I had been told the manuscript of these exercises had been procured by the Paris Opera Archives. This

I informed Olga, who was anxious for me to have them returned or have them copied. But after the curator had graciously given me permission to obtain copies I suddenly received, in July 1963, a letter from Spessivtzeva in Monte Carlo, where I was on holiday. "Do not bother to take or copy the exercises from the Paris Opera. I have written a new series, better, and I will give them to you on your return. Please hurry back to see me." Less than six months had passed since she found her liberty and was restored to the world. That I was happy to know her mind was again occupied with the dance is an understatement. I was overjoyed that she had not only found the time but the inclination to set down her wonderful exercises and so give to the world of dancers this knowledge and experience of her art.

It was at Arnold Haskell's happy suggestion that I first gave the manuscript to Joan Lawson, friend and fellow student of my early dancing days at Seraphine Astafieva's Russian Academy of Dancing, to read. She was enthusiastic from the start and her aid in analysing and going through the exercises minutely was indeed a labour of love. The exercises had been written in a mixture of Russian and French and, although perfectly clear to an advanced student, needed careful editing.

Only Joan Lawson and her great knowledge of the Academic dance could have achieved the result. More, she took the exercises to Leningrad and showed them to Natalia Dudinskaya of the Kirov Ballet. The latter, with the same enthusiasm, had her pupil pose for the series of pictures that illustrate so perfectly one of the adagios as set down by Olga Spessivtzeva.

The pupil is Valya Simoukova, who died tragically early in 1966 of a severe attack of measles and is mourned by her fellow students and her great teacher Natalia Dudinskaya. The photographer is Daniel Savelyev, a dancer of the Kirov's Corps de Ballet. To Joan Lawson, Natalia Dudinskaya and the two students, my grateful thanks and those of Olga Spessivtzeva, whose unique book of "Technique for the Ballet Artiste" awaits your approval.

A.D.

Monday

UNLESS OTHERWISE STATED ALL EXERCISES COMMENCE
FROM THE 5TH POSITION, R FOOT FRONT

1 *Grands Ronds de jambe en l'air* [Music, slow valse, 1 circle to each
   bar]
   8 times *en dehors* and 8 times *en dedans* (see note 1, page 63). Repeat
   opposite side.
   The arm is held in 2nd throughout (see note 2, page 63, for all arm
   positions and for the slight preparatory movement which
   precedes every exercise).

2 *Pliés* [Music, very slow valse, each *plié* taking 2 bars; or slow
   4/4 each *plié* taking 1 bar]

   2 *pliés* each in 1st, 2nd and 5th positions (2 with the R foot
   front and 2 with the R foot back). The head must anticipate
   the movement of the arm as it passes from 2nd to preparatory
   position and is raised through 1st back to 2nd.
                    Repeat to opposite side.

3 *Battements tendus* [Music, easy 2/4, each *battement* occupies 2
   beats, later 1 beat, the accent being on the outward movement]

   16 slow *battements tendus* moving alternately backwards and
   forwards (i.e. repeat sequence 8 times). Arm is held in 2nd and

11

there is a slight movement of the head to turn and incline towards the right on forwards movement and incline to left and turn to right on backwards movement.

32 quick *battements tendus* (moving as above) taking 1 beat for each movement and remaining absolutely still. Head and glance are forward, arm in 2nd. (These can also be performed *glissés*.)

Repeat to opposite side.

4   *Ronds de jambe à terre en dehors* [Music, 12 bars of slow 2/4]

8 slow *ronds de jambe à terre* (1 circle to each bar), the arm describes 2 simple *ports de bras* during these, moving from 2nd to preparatory position, up to 1st and back to 2nd.

8 quick *ronds de jambe à terre* (2 circles to each bar), arm remains still throughout. Close 5th *derrière*. Immediately rise on *demi-pointe* and open working leg *à la second* at 90°.

8 slow *petits ronds de jambe en l'air* (1 to each bar).

8 quick *ronds de jambe en l'air* (2 to each bar).

Arm is held in 2nd throughout these and head is turned towards working leg.

Repeat to opposite side.

Ronds de jambe à terre en dedans.

Repeat above sequence moving *en dedans*.

5   *Adagio* [Music, slow sarabande or valse]

Grands ronds de jambe en l'air en dehors. Commence from 5th with *développé en avant* through *tirebouchon* (see note 9, page 65) and circle at same height to *arabesque*, the arm moving through 1st to 2nd and then held (take 3 bars). During last bar of phrase, the working leg is swiftly circled to the front and back into *arabesque* before closing 5th *derrière*.

Repeat movement *en dedans*.

Repeat sequence 4 times in all before repeating to opposite side.

6   *Grands battements* [Music, strict 4/4 march, 2 beats to each *battement*, the accent being upwards on 1st and 3rd beat of each bar]

> 8 *Grands battements en avant.*
> 8 *Grands battements à la seconde* at 90°.
> 8 *Grands battements en arrière.*
> Arm is held in 2nd throughout and head straight.
> Repeat to opposite side.

7   *Petits battements sur le cou de pied* [Music, galop]

> 8 *petits battements sur le cou de pied* (supporting foot flat).
> 8 ditto (rising to *demi-pointe*) close 5th *derrière*.
> 8 *petits battements frappés en arrière* (supporting foot flat).
> 8 ditto (rising to *demi-pointe*) swiftly carry working foot forwards).
> 8 *petits battements frappés en avant* (supporting foot flat).
> 8 ditto (rising to *demi-pointe*).
> Repeat to opposite side.

CENTRE WORK

1   [Music, slow 4/4, sequence takes 8 bars] Commence 5th position, *en face*, arms opened in 2nd.

> 4 bars: 1 *battement tendu en avant* and 1 *battement tendu en arrière* repeated 4 times (take 2 beats for each *battement*).
> 2 bars: Repeat sequence 4 times quickly (1 beat to each *battement*).
> 1 bar: *Relevé* bringing working leg into *tirebouchon*, throw working leg outwards and fall into 2nd with *demi-plié*, 2 *pirouettes en dehors* on *demi-pointe*, raising working leg to *tirebouchon*; finish 4th position *croisé en arrière* in *demi-plié*.

13

1 bar: 3 *pirouttes en dehors*, working leg in *tirebouchon* and raise arms to 3rd position. Finish 5th *derrière en face* with arms still raised. (Opposite foot should now be ready to repeat sequence.) Drop arms to 2nd.

Repeat sequence 4 times in all.

2 [Music, slow 6/8, sequence takes 2 bars] Commence 5th *écarté*, travel forwards in a diagonal line.

Bar 1: *Coupé dessous* on to *demi-pointe* describing 2 *petits ronds de jambe en l'air en dehors* in 2nd. Close in 5th *devant* changing *épaulement* to *effacé*.
Bar 2: *Piqué* into 2nd *arabesque* (see note 3, page 64) *fondu* holding *arabesque*.
Repeat sequence 4 times in all before repeating to opposite side.

3 [Music, slow 6/8, sequence takes 2 bars] This exercise is the reverse of No. 2 and moves backwards along a diagonal line. Commence 5th position *écarté*.

Bar 1: *Coupé dessus* on to *demi-pointe* and describe 2 *petits ronds de jambe en l'air en dedans* in 2nd. Close in 5th *derrière* changing *épaulement* to *effacé*.
Bar 2: *Piqué* into 4th *en l'air, fondu* holding pose. Repeat sequence 4 times in all before repeating to opposite side.

4 [Music, 3/4, mazurka moderato, sequence takes 4 bars] Commence 5th position *croisé*.

Bar 1: 3 *coupés* (i.e. *dessous, dessus, dessous*).
Bar 2: 1 *battement frappé* (i.e. take working foot from front to back). Drop in 4th position *croisé* with *demi-plié*.
Bar 3: 1 *pirouette en dehors* (raised foot *sur le cou de pied devant*). Drop raised foot into 4th position *croisé en arrière*.

Bar 4: *Demi-plié* and 4 *pirouettes en dedans* with raised foot *sur le cou de pied derrière*. Finish closing raised foot 5th *derrière*. Repeat sequence to opposite side.

Repeat sequence 4 times in all.

5 [Music, march-like 4/4, sequence takes 2 bars] Commence 5th position *croisé*.

Bar 1: 2 *relevés* on *demi-pointe*, working foot *sur le cou de pied devant*. Close 5th position *devant* in *demi-plié*.
Bar 2: 1 *changement des pieds* changing *épaulement* to *croisé* on opposite side. *Relevé* raising working leg to *attitude en avant* (i.e. L leg is raised). Finish closing 5th *devant*. Repeat to opposite side.

Repeat sequence 4 times in all.

ADAGIO

1 [Music, slow valse taking 2 bars for each *retiré*; sequence takes 16 bars] Commence 5th position *croisé*. Sequence is performed on *demi-pointe* throughout.

Raising L arm to 3rd and R arm in 2nd, raise R leg slowly to *tirebouchon*, then lower it slowly into 5th *derrière*.
Repeat bringing R leg from back to front. Repeat this movement 4 times in all; lower heels and change *épaulement* on the last of these. Change arms, rise to *demi-pointes* and repeat to opposite side.

2 [Music, sarabande, each sequence takes 8 bars] Commence 5th position *en face*, whole exercise is performed on *demi-pointes*.

Bar 1: Slowly raise working leg into 2nd position *à la seconde* at 90°, opening R arm to 3rd and L arm to 2nd.

Bars 2 and 3: Bring working leg into *tirebouchon* then open slowly into *développé en avant*.

Bar 4: Bring working leg back to *tirebouchon*.

Bars 5, 6, 7: Slowly open working leg into *arabesque*, hold.

Bar 8: Slowly lower leg to 5th *derrière*.

Once arms have reached above position they remain still until foot closes at end of sequence. Repeat sequence to opposite side.

Repeat sequence 4 times in all.

3 [Music, slow valse, take 4 bars for each *développé*, whole sequence takes 32 bars] Commence 5th position *effacé*, exercise is performed on *demi-pointes* throughout.

Slow *développé* to *arabesque* passing R arm to 3rd and L arm to 2nd position. Close 5th position *derrière*. Repeat this *développé* 4 times with L leg.

ALLEGRO

1 [Music, 2/4, sequence takes 16 bars] Commence 2nd position *en face*, the *sauts* and *relevés* are performed upwards on the beat.

8 *sauts* in 2nd position using *demi-pliés* between each.

8 ditto without *demi-pliés*.

8 *relevés* in 2nd using *demi-pliés* between each.

8 *relevés* without *demi-pliés*.

Repeat sequence using 1st position.

2 [Music, 2/4 allegretto, sequence takes 4 bars] Commence 5th position *en face*.

4 *assemblés dessus*, travelling forwards, using natural *épaulement* (see notes 4 and 7, page 64 and 65), using *pliés* between each.

1 *assemblé dessus*, travelling sideways, closing 5th *plié*.
Relevé sur les pointes. Repeat *assemblé dessus* and *relevé* to opposite side.

Repeat sequence 4 times in all.

Repeat entire sequence using *assemblé dessous*.

3   [Music, easy 2/4, sequence takes 4 bars] Commence 5th position *en face*.

4 *jetés devant* describing a *rond de jambe en dehors* each *jeté*.
4 *jetés dessous* describing *rond de jambe en dedans* on *jeté*.
Use natural *épaulement* throughout (see note 7, page 65).

Repeat whole sequence twice in all.

4   [Music, grande valse, sequence takes 8 bars] Commence 5th position *écarté*.

Bar 1: *Glissade derrière* (see note 5, page 64), *grand assemblé dessus*.
Bar 2: *Failli en tournant*, finishing 1st *arabesque effacé*.
Bars 3 and 4: Hold *arabesque*, then close raised leg 5th *derrière*.
Bar 5: *Failli* passing raised leg through 1st to 5th position *croisé*.
Bar 6: *Coupé dessous*.
Bars 7 and 8: *Grand assemblé en avant*. Hold 5th position with R arm in 3rd and L in 2nd position.

Repeat twice in all.

Repeat to opposite side.

5   [Music, grande valse, sequence takes 4 bars] Travelling in a diagonal line commence back to line of dance, R *pointe dégagé en arrière*.

Pas courus (i.e. 3 running steps) as preparation for *grand jeté entrelacé; assemblé en arrière; sissonne ouverte* into *attitude effacé,* raising R arm in 3rd and L in 2nd.

Repeat 4 times in all before repeating to opposite side.

6   [Music, quick 4/4] Commence 5th position *en face.*

Echappé into 2nd *en face,* close 5th position *croisé.*
2 *entrechats quatre.*
Repeat 4 times on alternate feet, slightly opening the arms from preparatory position on each *échappé.*

7   [Music, strong valse, sequence takes 4 bars] Commence 4th position *croisé,* L *pointe dégagé en arrière.*

Assemblé en arrière and with a strong upward jump on L describe 2 *petits ronds de jambe en l'air* with R. Jump again on L, bringing R into *tirebouchon* whilst changing *épaulement.* Finish 4th position *croisé,* R *pointe dégagé en arrière.*
Repeat 8 times in all.

8   [Music, à six temps] Commence 5th *en face.*

3 *entrechats six, relevé sur la pointe* into *attitude* raising both arms to 3rd. Hold. Then lower raised leg to 5th position *derrière* and arms through 2nd to preparatory position.
Repeat 8 times in all.

9   [Music, slow sustained 4/4, sequence taking 1 bar, or valse, sequence taking 2 bars] Commence 5th position *en face.*

Glissade dessous, closing 5th, *relevé sur les pointes,* arms open to *demi-seconde* with *glissade* and close to preparatory position with *relevé.*

Repeat 8 times with *glissade dessous*, then repeat 8 times with *glissade dessus*, raising arms to 3rd on *relevé*. Use natural *épaulement* throughout.

10 [Music, mazurka moderato, sequence takes 1 bar] Commence 4th position *croisé*, L *pointe dégagé en arrière*.
Coupé dessous; *ballonné en avant*, turning *effacé*; *ballonné en avant* travelling well forwards but closing R foot *sur le cou de pied derrière* and changing *épaulement* to *croisé* on opposite side. Repeat to opposite side.
Repeat sequence 8 times in all.

PORTS DE BRAS

[Music, slow valse] Commence 1st position *en face*.

Bar 1: Bend forwards as far as possible entirely relaxing upper half of body and dropping arms to the ground.
Bar 2: Raise arms to 5th, straightening body.
Bars 3 and 4: Bend backwards as far as possible from waist upwards; rise and open arms to 2nd position.
Bars 5 and 6: Bend sideways to left, raising R arm to 3rd, leaving L in 2nd. Straighten returning arm to 2nd.
Bars 7 and 8: Bend sideways to right, raising L arm to 3rd, leaving R in 2nd. Straighten returning arm to 2nd.
Repeat *ports de bras* 4 times in all.

Tuesday

BARRE-WORK

1   Repeat Monday's exercise 1, *Grands ronds de jambe.*

2   *Pliés* [Music, slow valse]

1 *plié* taking 3 bars, and 1 *plié* taking 1 bar.
Repeat this sequence in 1st, 2nd and 5th *devant* and 5th *derrière*,
using the arm and head as in Monday's exercise 2.
Repeat to opposite side.

3   *Battements tendus en croix* [Music, an easy 2/4]

4 sets *battements tendus en croix*, taking 1 bar to each *battement*
the accent is outwards on 1st beat.
2 sets *battements glissés (jetés) en croix*, taking 1 beat to each
battement and closing in 1st position.
8 *battements glissés (jetés)* passing from front to back through 1st,
close last in 5th position *derrière*.
Arm held in 2nd position throughout.
Repeat to opposite side.

4   *Ronds de jambe à terre* [Music, slow 6/8]

2 slow and 3 quick *ronds de jambe à terre*, repeat 4 times *en dehors*,
and 4 times *en dedans*. Then repeat sequence at same tempo
using *petits ronds de jambe en l'air*, twice on flat supporting foot,
and twice on *demi-pointe*. Arm is held in 2nd throughout.
Repeat to opposite side.

5   *Adagio* [Music, slow valse or minuet, taking 4 bars for each *développé*]

Développé en avant (supporting foot flat, *retiré* into *tirebouchon* rising to *demi-pointe*).
Repeat this *développé* twice *en avant*, twice *à la seconde* at 90°, twice into *arabesque*, and twice *à la seconde* at 90°.
The arm completes a full *ports de bras* with each *développé*.
Repeat to opposite side.

6   *Battements fondus* [Music, smooth 6/8]

1 *battement fondu en avant* and (changing legs) 1 *battement fondu en arrière* repeated twice. Working foot does not leave the floor and movement passes through flat supporting foot. Arms in 2nd.
Repeat above sequence twice, just raising foot from floor and passing movement through *demi-pointe*.
Continue with 1 *battement fondu en avant* and 1 *battement fondu en arrière*, raising leg slightly higher and through *demi-pointe*.
1 slow *battement fondu en avant* raised to 90°, supporting leg in deep *fondu*, 1 slow *battement fondu en arrière* into high *arabesque*. (During these 2 *battements*, the arm describes a full *ports de bras*.)
6 quick *battements fondus en avant* and *en arrière* passing through *demi-pointes*. Arm is in 2nd.
Coupé dessus to face *barre* and holding with both hands perform 8 *battements fondus à la seconde* on alternate feet passing through 1st position.
Repeat to opposite side.

CENTRE WORK

1   [Music, steady 2/4, sequence takes 8 bars] Commence 5th position *croisé*.

8 *battements tendus en avant en tournant,* using arms as follows:
1. L in 1st, R in 2nd; 2. both in 2nd; 3. L in 1st, R in 2nd;
4. both in 2nd; 5. R in 1st, L in 2nd; 6. both in 2nd; 7. R in 1st,
L in 2nd; 8. both in 2nd. (Take 2 beats for each *battement.*)
8 quick *battements glissés* (*jetés*) *en avant en face* (1 beat to each
battement). Glide from foot into 4th position *croisé* and *demi-plié.*
2 *pirouettes en dehors en tirebouchon* (turn to left picking up back
foot) closing 5th position *derrière.*
3 *pirouettes en dedans* (turning to right picking up back foot)
closing 5th position *devant.* Repeat to opposite side.
Repeat sequence twice in all.

2   *Ronds de jambe en tournant en dehors* [Music, slow valse sequence
takes 16 bars] Commence 5th position *en face* in *demi-plié.*

Bars 1 and 2: *Développé en avant,* rise on *demi-pointe* and make
$\frac{1}{4}$ turn *en dehors,* carrying working leg into 2nd at 90°, lower
heel.
Bars 3 and 4: Rise on *demi-pointe* and perform 2 *petits ronds de
jambe en l'air en dehors,* pass raised leg into *tirebouchon,* lowering
heel of supporting leg and *fondu.*
Repeat this movement 4 times in all and, having returned *en
face,* close raised leg in 5th *derrière.*
Repeat sequence on opposite leg.

3   *Ronds de jambe en tournant en dedans* [Music as for above]

Repeat exercise 2, commencing *développé en arrière,* turning *en
dedans* and using *petits ronds de jambe en l'air en dedans.*

4   [Music, easy 2/4, sequence takes 4 bars] Travelling diagonally
forwards, commence 5th position *écarté.*

Coupé dessous on to *demi-pointe,* 3 *battements frappés* (passing

derrière, devant, derrière). On 4th *battement frappé* drop into *fondu*
and bring working leg *sur le cou de pied devant*, changing
épaulement to *effacé*; *piqué* into 1 *pirouette en attitude en dedans*,
finish *effacé* on *fondu* and hold *attitude*. *Coupé* changing
épaulement.

Repeat 4 times in all.

Repeat sequence to opposite side.

5 [Music, easy 2/4 as above, sequence takes 4 bars] Travelling
diagonally backwards, commence 5th position *croisé*.

Coupé dessous on to *demi-pointe*, 3 *petits battements sur le cou de
pied*, on 4th *battement* pass working foot through *tirebouchon* to
finish *sur le cou de pied derrière*, changing *épaulement* to *effacé* with
fondu on supporting leg. *Piqué en arrière* into 1 *pirouette en
attitude en avant en dehors*; finish *croisé* on *fondu* and hold
attitude. *Coupé*.

Repeat 4 times in all.

Repeat to opposite side.

ADAGIO

1 [Music, sarabande or slow minuet, sequence takes 4 bars]
Commence 5th position *sur les demi-pointes*.
Bar 1: Slow *développé en avant*, opening both arms into 2nd.
Bar 2: Fall into 4th position *en avant* in *fondu*, leaving L *pointe
dégagé en arrière*, raising L arm to 3rd, and leaving R arm in 2nd,
bend body and head forwards.
Bar 3: Transfer weight on to L foot, bending body and head
slightly backwards.
Bar 4: Rise on L *demi-pointe* and slowly *développé* R *en avant*,
leaving arms as before. Bring raised leg back into 5th *sur les
demi-pointes*.

Repeat 4 times in all on alternate legs.

2   [Music as for 1st *adagio*] Commence 5th *en face sur les demi-pointes*.

Slow *développé à la seconde*, raising R arm to 3rd and L to 2nd. Fall into 2nd position *fondu*, L *pointe dégagé à la seconde à terre*, raising L arm to 3rd and dropping R into 2nd, and bending body and head sideways to right. Straighten body and step on to L *demi-pointe*, *développé* R *à la seconde* at 90°, changing arms. Bring R leg back to 5th *derrière sur les demi-pointes*.
        Repeat 4 times in all on alternate legs.

3   [Music as for 1st *adagio*] Commence 5th *effacé sur les demi-pointes*.

Repeat movement as in *Adagio* 1, reversing movements, i.e. *développé* into 2nd *arabesque*, fall into 4th *en arrière (effacé)*, raising L arm into 3rd and R into 2nd.
        Repeat 4 times in all on alternate legs.

ALLEGRO

1   [Music, easy 6/8, whole sequence takes 8 bars] Commence 5th position *en face*.

1 *assemblé battu devant*, 1 *assemblé battu dessous*. (N.B. *Assemblé battu devant* in the Russian school is performed thus: glide front foot upwards and outwards with a strong jump upwards and forwards on left, beat R in front of L and return to floor, both feet together, R foot 5th *devant*. *Assemblé battu derrière* reverses this movement.) See below.
        Repeat 4 times in all using alternate feet.
Now reverse this movement, i.e. 1 *assemblé battu derrière*, 1 *assemblé battu dessus*.
        Repeat 4 times in all using alternate feet.
(N.B. The first sequence should travel backwards, the second forwards.)

2   [Music, easy 2/4, sequence requires 12 bars] Commence 2nd position *en face*. (*Relevé* on 1st beat, *demi-plié* on second beat of each bar.)

8 slow *relevés sur les pointes*, with strong *demi-pliés* between each. 8 quick *relevés*, raising working leg to *tirebouchon en avant*, returning to 2nd position between each. (Take 1 beat for each *relevé*.)

      Repeat whole sequence 4 times in all.

3   [Music, easy 2/4, sequence takes 16 bars] Commence 5th position *en face*.

1 *jeté battement en arrière*. 1 *temps levé*.

      Repeat 8 times in all on alternate feet.

1 *jeté battement en avant*, 1 *temps levé*.

      Repeat 8 times in all on alternate feet.

4   [Music, valse, sequence takes 4 bars] Travelling diagonally forwards, commence 4th position *croisé* in slight *demi-plié*.

Bar 1: *Glissade en avant* (see note 6, page 64).
Bar 2: *Grand jeté en avant* into 2nd *arabesque*.
Bar 3: *Relevé* on *demi-pointes* and with a brush along floor (Russian *flak*) pass working leg through 1st position into *attitude en avant*, raising both arms to 3rd.
Bar 4: Fall into 4th position *croisé* with slight *demi-plié*.

      Repeat sequence 4 times.
      Repeat to opposite side.

5   [Music, mazurka, sequence takes 4 bars] Travelling diagonally backwards, commence 5th position *effacé*.

Sissonne à pointe en arrière (*Sissonne relevé*), i.e. spring backwards on to *pointe* of supporting leg, raising working leg into *tirebouchon en avant*, or *attitude en avant*. Arm on same side as raised foot is in 1st, the other is in 2nd. Close 5th position *devant*.

Repeat 4 times in all.

Repeat to opposite side, then reverse movement, i.e. *Sissonne à pointe en avant (Sissonne relevée)*, i.e. spring forwards on to *pointe*, raising working leg *en arrière* to *attitude* or *arabesque*, arm on opposite side to raised foot in 1st, other in 2nd. Close 5th position *derrière*.

Repeat 4 times in all.

Repeat to opposite side.

6   [Music, valse, sequence takes 4 bars. 1 movement is taken to each bar] Commence 5th position *effacé*.

Coupé dessous, ballonné en avant, temps levé describing *demi-rond de jambe en l'air en dehors* and finishing *attitude effacé* (supporting leg in *fondu*) with same arm in 3rd as leg raised, other in 2nd. Hold. Repeat to opposite side.

Repeat sequence 4 times in all.

Repeat 4 times stepping on to full *pointe*, i.e. *coupé dessous* on to *pointe*, jump on *pointe*, etc. (For this sequence the music changes to slow mazurka.)

Then repeat reversing the movement, i.e. *Coupé dessus, ballonné en arrière, temps levé* describing *demi-rond de jambe en dedans*, finishing *attitude effacé en avant* with opposite arm raised in 3rd to leg raised, etc.

7   [Music, quick 6/8, 2 *entrechats* in each bar] Commence 5th position *en face sur les pointes*.

8 *entrechats sixes* without descending from *les pointes*.

8   [Music, galop, sequence takes 16 bars] Commence 4th position

croisé. The first part of this exercise is performed without the raised leg falling to the floor.

Bars 1–3: 6 *sauts* in 1st *arabesque en tournant en dehors* (supporting leg in good *fondu*)
Bar 4: 1 *pirouette en dehors*, bringing raised leg into *tirebouchon* and opening it again to *arabesque en face*, supporting leg *fondu*.
Bar 5: 2 *pirouettes en dehors*.
Bars 6–13: Repeat single and double *pirouettes* 4 times in all.
Bars 14–16: Drop raised leg and travel diagonally forwards with 6 *emboités en tournant* (*petits jetés*), both arms opened in 2nd.
Repeat to opposite side.

9   [Music 2/4, sequence takes 16 bars. *Relevé* on 1st beat and close in 5th position on 2nd beat]

8 *relevés passés en arrière*.
8 *relevés passés en avant*.
Repeat sequence twice in all, using natural *épaulement*.

PORTS DE BRAS

Repeat as for Monday's *Ports de bras*, but place the feet in 5th position and change front foot at the commencement of each sequence.

Wednesday

BARRE-WORK

1 *Grands ronds de jambe en l'air en dehors*

Repeat first part only of Monday's exercise 1.

2 *Pliés* [Music, slow 4/4, 1 *plié* to each bar]

2 *pliés* each in 1st, 2nd and 5th position *devant*. *Battement tendu à côté*, drop heel to floor; raise heel and return to working foot to 5th *derrière*, then repeat *battement tendu* closing working foot 5th position *devant*.
Repeat *battement tendu* 16 times in all and continue with 3 quick *battements glissés* (*jetés*) into 5th position. On 4th *battement*, *relevé* on *demi-pointe*, raising working leg *à la seconde* at 90°.
Repeat last sequence with *battements glissés* 4 times in all.
Repeat to opposite side.

3 *Pliés* in 4th with *ronds de jambe en l'air* [Music, valse, taking 2 bars to each *plié* and 1 bar to each *petit rond de jambe*]

Plié in 4th, as the legs straighten carrying working leg *en dehors à la seconde*; 2 *petits ronds de jambe en l'air en dehors*. Pass working leg through 1st back to 4th position.
Repeat this sequence 4 times slowly in all and 4 times quickly.
Repeat to opposite side.
Repeat reversing movement, i.e. using *ronds de jambe en dedans*.

4 *Petits ronds de jambe en l'air* [Music, easy 2/4]

2 *petits ronds de jambe en l'air en dehors* (supporting foot flat).
2 ditto, rising to *demi-pointe*.
Repeat this sequence 4 times slowly and 4 times quickly.
Fondu on supporting leg, bringing working leg *en avant*.
2 *pirouettes en dehors*, finishing 5th position *derrière*.
Repeat sequence reversing movement, i.e. *petits ronds de jambe en dedans* and 2 *pirouettes en dedans*.
Repeat to opposite side.

5 *Adagio* [Music, slow valse, sarabande, or minuet, taking 4 bars to each *développé*, sequence takes 32 bars]

Développé en avant, rise on *demi-pointe*, balance and close 5th *devant*, lowering heels.
Repeat *développé à la seconde*, into *arabesque* and again *à la seconde*. Repeat this sequence twice in all. The arm describes a full *ports de bras* with each *développé*.
(Quicken tempo and take 2 bars to each movement from front to back.)
8 *grands battements en balançoire*, passing working leg through *tirebouchon* and not through 1st position *à terre*. Arm is held in 2nd position throughout.
Repeat to opposite side.

6 *Battements fondus à la seconde* [Music, valse, each *battement* takes 2 bars]

2 *battements fondus à la seconde*.
4 *petits battements sur le cou de pied*. (Each *battement* takes 1 bar.)
Repeat 4 times in all.
Repeat to opposite side.

7 *Battements frappés* [Music, 4/4 march, sequence takes 16 bars]

4 *battements frappés* from *sur le cou de pied*, opening to 2nd with accent outwards (supporting foot flat).
4 ditto, rising to *demi-pointe*.

Repeat 4 times in all.
Repeat to opposite side.

CENTRE PRACTICE

1   *Temps liés* [Music, valse, minuet or sarabande, 1 *temps lié* takes 4 bars] The movement must be absolutely continuous throughout. Commence 5th position *croisé*, arms in preparatory position, head inclined over L shoulder.

Bar 1: *Glissé en avant*, leaving L *pointe dégagé en arrière*, raising L arm to 3rd, opening R to 2nd and turning head to right.
Bar 2: Close 5th *derrière*, dropping L arm to 1st and bringing head *en face*, glance downwards, *demi-plié*.
Bar 3: *Glissé* R foot *à la seconde*, leaving L *pointe dégagé à côté*, opening L arm to 2nd and turning head to left.
Bar 4: Close L foot 5th position *devant*, changing *épaulement* to opposite side, dropping both arms to preparatory position and inclining head over right shoulder. *Demi-plié* and repeat sequence to opposite side.

Repeat sequence 4 times in all.
Repeat reversing all movement, i.e.

Temps lié en arrière.
The arms can also move into 2nd *arabesque, arabesque à deux bras, attitude*, etc.

2   [Music, quick 4/4, sequence takes 4 bars] Commence 5th position *en face*.

8 quick *battements tendus à côté* on alternate feet, closing 5th *derrière*, arms in *demi-seconde* and using natural *épaulement*.

Repeat closing 5th position *devant*.

Repeat sequence twice in all.

3 [Music, slow 4/4, sequence takes 2 bars] Commence 4th position *croisé* L foot *pointe dégagé en arrière*. Commence exercise on anacrusis.

Coupé dessous on to *demi-pointe* and raising working foot *sur le cou de pied devant*.

Bar 1: 3 *battements frappés*, lower heel changing *épaulement* to *effacé*.

Bar 2: Rise to *demi-pointe*, throwing working leg into *battement jeté en avant*, raising L arm in 3rd and opening R to 2nd; fall on to raised leg, dropping L arm into 1st; *coupé dessous* and *chassé en avant* into 2nd *arabesque*, supporting leg *fondu*.

Repeat 4 times in all.

Repeat to opposite side.

4 [Music, easy 2/4, sequence takes 4 bars] Commence 4th position *croisé* R foot *pointe dégagé en avant*. Commence on anacrusis.

Coupé dessus (on to R *demi-pointe*), changing *épaulement* to *effacé* and raising L foot *sur le cou de pied derrière*.

Bars 1 and 2: 3 *petits battements sur le cou de pied*, drop heel; rise on *demi-pointe*, and throw L leg into *battement jeté en arrière*, raising L arm to 3rd and opening R to 2nd.

Bar 3: Bring L leg into *tirebouchon*; *chassé en arrière* (L foot); *coupé dessus*.

Bar 4: *Piqué* on to L *demi-pointe*, raising R into *attitude effacé en avant*; raising L arm into 3rd and opening R into 2nd.

Repeat 4 times in all.

Repeat to opposite side.

5   [Music, à six temps] Commence 5th position *croisé sur les pointes* or *demi-pointes* and do not descend throughout the exercises.

3 *petits battements sur le cou de pied.* Close 5th *devant, grand changement des pieds,* changing *épaulement* to opposite side.
Repeat sequence 8 times in all.

ADAGIO

[Music, sarabande, minuet, sequence takes 8 bars] Commence 5th position *en face.*

1   Bar 1: *Plié* in 5th, arms in preparatory position.
Bar 2: 2 *pirouettes en dehors,* finishing *en face à la seconde* at 90°.
Bars 3 and 4: Turn into 1st *arabesque,* hold, close 5th position *derrière* in *demi-plié,* body bending slightly forwards; *Sissonne ouverte* into 1st *arabesque* taking arms upwards through 1st to 3rd and opening to 2nd; hold on *fondu,* close 5th position *derrière.*
Bar 5: *Temps levé* into *arabesque,* arms opening to 2nd and pass, working foot through 1st to 4th position *croisé en avant.*
Bar 6: *Piqué* on to back foot (i.e. L) and 2 *pirouettes en dedans,* finishing in *attitude en face.* (Supporting leg *fondu,* place raised foot 4th *en arrière.* This is merely a stretching movement into *dégagé,* but the toe scarcely touches the floor.)
Bars 7 and 8: 3 *pirouettes en dedans,* during the third of these incline body sideways towards supporting leg, raising same arm as leg raised into 3rd, stretching the other forwards into 1st; finish by opening raised leg *à la seconde* at 90° and raising both arms to 3rd. Close 5th position *derrière* and repeat to opposite side.
Repeat sequence 4 times in all on alternate legs.

2   [Music, valse, the timing of this exercise can vary considerably that given is only a suggestion] Commence 4th position *croisé*, L *pointe dégagé en arrière*, L arm in 3rd, R in 2nd.

Bars 1–4: *Ports de bras*, i.e. drop L arm into preparatory position; raise L to 2nd, dropping R into preparatory position; raise R to 3rd; *fondu* on R leg, taking R arm through 2nd to 1st as preparation for:

Bars 5–8: 2 *pirouettes en dedans* in 1st *arabesque*, finishing in 3rd *arabesque* (i.e. *croisé* and *fondu* on supporting leg); *relevé* into *attitude croisé*; lower raised leg into 4th *croisé en arrière* and *pointe tendue*.

Bars 1–4: Repeat *ports de bras* as above.

Bars 5–8: Take preparation and 2 *pirouettes en dedans en attitude*, finish in *attitude croisé*. (*Fondu* on supporting leg; *relevé* in *attitude*, lower raised leg into 4th *croisé en arrière* and *pointe tendue*.)

Bars 1–4: Repeat *ports de bras* as above.

Bars 5–8: Take preparation and 3 *pirouettes en tirebouchon en dedans*; during the third of these bend body towards raised leg, raising same arm in 3rd as raised leg and closing other in 1st; finish by extending raised leg *à la seconde* at 90°, both arms in 3rd. This should be held on *demi-pointe*.

Repeat to opposite side.

Repeat sequence 4 times in all on alternate feet.

ALLEGRO

1   [Music, 2/4 or light 6/8, sequence takes 8 bars of 2/4 or 4 bars of 6/8] Commence 5th position *en face*.

8 *assemblés battus dessous* followed by 8 *assemblés battus dessus*. Movement should travel backwards and then equally forwards using natural *épaulement*, the arms opening lightly sideways as legs descend and closing into preparatory position as feet close in 5th position.

2 [Music, easy 2/4 or 6/8. Whole sequence takes 8 bars of 2/4 or 4 bars of 6/8]

8 *jetés battements devant.*
8 *jetés battements derrière.*
See note above for arms and *épaulement.*

3 [Music, mazurka, sequence takes 2 bars] Commence 5th position *croisé.*

Bar 1 beats 1–2: *Brisé en avant* (see note 8, page 65), hold 5th position in *demi-plié*; beat 3: *Sissonne fermée dessus.*
Bar 2 beats 1–2: *Brisé en arrière*, hold 5th position in *demi-plié*; beat 3: *Sissonne fermée dessous.*
Repeat sequence 4 times to each side, using natural *épaulement.*

4 [Music, easy 6/8] Commence 5th position *en face.*

Gargouillade en dehors to right, repeat to left.
Entrechat quatre, Royale. (Changement battu.)
Repeat to opposite side.
Repeat 8 times in all.

5 [Music, slow mazurka, or 3/4, sequence takes 2 bars] Commence 5th position *effacé*, travel diagonally forwards.

Bar 1: *Glissade en avant* (see note 6, p. 64; 2nd step is a preparation). *Cabriole en avant*, raising L arm to 3rd and opening R to 2nd.
Bar 2: *Jeté en avant* into 2nd *arabesque*; *petit jeté en arrière.*
Repeat 4 times in all.
Repeat to opposite side.

6 [Music, valse] Commence 4th position *effacé*, L *pointe dégagé en arrière.*

Bar 1: *Pas courus en arrière* (i.e. 3 running steps backwards, the last being a preparation for *cabriole*).

Bar 2: *Cabriole en avant en tournant*, finishing in 4th *arabesque* (see note 3, page 64), supporting leg *fondu*.

Bar 3: *Pas de bourrés en avant*, the last step passing into 4th and *piqué en avant* into 1st *arabesque*.

Bar 4: Fall back on to raised leg and *cabriole en avant*, raising both arms to 1st.

Repeat to opposite side.

Repeat sequence 4 times in all.

7   [Music, 2/4, sequence takes 16 bars] Commence 5th position *en face*.

8 slow *échappés à la seconde sur les pointes* with good *plié* in 5th position between each.

16 quick *échappés à la seconde sur les pointes* with no *plié* between each.

Repeat sequence twice in all.

8   [Music, 2/4, single sequence takes 4 bars] Commence 5th position *en face*.

Piqué travelling backwards and bringing R *sur le cou de pied devant*, close 5th position *demi-plié*.

Piqué travelling sideways and opening L leg *à la seconde* at 45°, close 5th position *derrière*, *demi-plié*.

Piqué travelling forwards, bring L *sur le cou de pied derrière*, close 5th position *derrière demi-plié*.

Piqué travelling sideways, opening R leg *à la seconde* at 45°, close 5th position *derrière*, *demi-plié*.

Repeat on opposite side.

Repeat sequence 8 times in all.

9   [Music, 2/4, sequence takes 8 bars] Commence 5th position *effacé*, travelling diagonally forwards.

8 *soubresauts*, jumping forwards *sur les pointes*.
8 *soubresauts* (having descended from *les pointes*), jumping well forwards and bending the knees at the height of each jump. L arm is in 3rd and R arm in 2nd. Hands are opened facing each other.

Repeat to opposite side.

10   [Music, 6/8, sequence takes 2 bars] Commence 4th position *croisé*, L foot *pointe dégagé*.

Ballotté en avant, changing *épaulement* to *effacé*. (Both feet must meet in 5th position *en l'air* during the jump.)
Ballotté en arrière, keeping *épaulement effacé*. (Both feet meeting in 5th *en l'air* during jump.)
Coupé dessous, changing *épaulement* to *en face*.
Ballonné à la seconde at 90°, changing *épaulement* to *croisé*.

Repeat sequence to opposite side.

Repeat sequence 8 times in all.

11   [Music, 4/4] Commence 5th position *en face*.

1 *grand battement à la seconde* at 90° (closing 5th *devant*).
1 *Rond de jambe à terre en dehors*, closing 5th *derrière*.

Repeat 8 times in all on alternate feet.

1 *grand battement à la seconde* at 90°, closing 5th *derrière*.
1 *Rond de jambe à terre en dedans*, closing 5th *devant*.

Repeat sequence 8 times in all on alternate feet.

PORTS DE BRAS

Repeat as for Monday's *Ports de bras*.

Thursday

BARRE-WORK

1   Repeat Monday's first exercise.

2   *Pliés* [Music, valse or 4/4]

    2 *pliés* each in 1st, 2nd, 5th position *devant* and 5th position *derrière*, arms and head performing the usual *ports de bras*.

3   *Battements tendus* and *battements glissés* [Music, 2/4]

    16 *battements tendus à côté*, closing alternatively 5th *devant* and 5th *derrière* (2 beats to each *battement*).
    16 *battements glissés à côté*, ditto (1 beat to each *battement*).

4   *Ronds de jambe à terre* [Music, 4/4]

    2 *ronds de jambe à terre en dehors*.
    2 *petits ronde de jambe en l'air en dehors à la seconde*, rising to *demi-pointe* on supporting leg.
    Repeat sequence twice slowly and twice quickly, continue:
    1 *grand rond de jambe à terre en dehors* (supporting leg in good *fondu*). Hold *pointe dégagé en arrière*, bend body forwards and then backwards, describing full *ports de bras*.
          Repeat to opposite side.
          Repeat sequence *en dedans*.

5   *Adagio* [Music, sarabande or minuet]

Raise and hold working leg *en avant, demi-rond de jambe en dehors à la seconde* at 90°; 1 slow *petit rond de jambe en l'air en dehors,* return leg *en avant.*
Repeat this sequence 4 times in all before closing raised leg 5th position *derrière.*
Repeat reversing movement, i.e. raise leg to *arabesque* and move *en dedans.*
Repeat to opposite side.

6   *Grands battements* [Music, march 4/4]

8 *grands battements* from *pointe dégagé en avant,* closing last 5th position *devant.*
8 *grands battements* from *pointe dégagé à la seconde,* closing last in 5th position *derrière.*
8 *grands battements* from *pointe dégagé en arrière,* closing last in 5th position *derrière.*
8 *grands battements* from *pointe dégagé à la seconde,* closing last 5th position *derrière.*
Repeat to opposite side.

7   *Petits battements sur le cou de pied* [Music, galop]

4 *petits battements sur le cou de pied* (supporting foot flat).
4 ditto (rising to *demi-pointe*) and finishing *pointe dégagé à la seconde.*
Repeat sequence commencing with working foot *sur le cou de pied derrière.*
Repeat sequence twice in all.
Repeat on opposite side.

8   *Battements fondus* [Music, slow 4/4]

1 *battement fondu*, moving from *sur le cou de pied devant à la seconde* and closing *sur le cou de pied derrière*.
1 *battement fondu* reversing movement.

Repeat above 8 times in all.

16 *battements fondus en croix* (supporting foot flat).
16 ditto, rising to *demi-pointe* and passing through 5th position with each *battement*.

Repeat on opposite side.

CENTRE PRACTICE

1 [Music, 4/4, sequence requires 8 bars] Commence 5th *en face*.

Battements tendus en croix, 2 sets taking 2 beats to each *battement* and 2 sets taking only 1 beat.
Coupé dessous on to *demi-pointe*, opening working *à la seconde* at 90°.
2 *petits ronds de jambe en l'air en dehors*.
Flic-flac en dehors, finishing with working leg *à la seconde* on *demi-pointe*. Close 5th position *derrière*.

Repeat to opposite side.

Repeat reversing sequence, i.e. use *petits ronds de jambe en l'air en dedans* and *flic-flac en dedans*.

2 [Music, slow 4/4, sequence takes 2 bars] Commence 5th position *en face*.

Bar 1: *Coupé dessous* on to *demi-pointe*, 3 *battements frappés*, the third finishing *sur le cou de pied derrière* and supporting leg *fondu*.
Bar 2: 3 *pirouettes en dehors*, finishing with raised leg in *tirebouchon devant en face*, fall into 4th position *en avant*, *demi-plié*, 3 *pirouettes en dedans*, finishing by falling *en avant* on to raised leg and other foot *sur le cou de pied derrière*.

Repeat to opposite side.
Repeat 4 times in all on alternate feet.

3   [Music, 4/4, sequence takes 2 bars] Commence 5th position *en face*.

Bar 1: *Coupé dessous, 3 petits battements sur le cou de pied, fondu.*
Bar 2: Rise to *demi-pointe* and open working leg *à la seconde* at 90°, hold; drop working leg and *demi-plié* in 2nd position.
Repeat on opposite side.
Repeat 4 times in all on alternate feet.

ADAGIO

1   [Music slow valse, sarabande, sequence takes 16 bars] Commence 4th position *croisé*. R *pointe dégagé en arrière.*

Bars 1–4: *Assemblé en arrière* to 5th; *demi-plié*, 2 *pirouettes en dehors*, finishing in *attitude croisé.*
Bars 5–8: Still turning *en dehors*, bring working leg to *tirebouchon*, finishing *en face* by opening working leg *à la seconde* at 90°.
Bars 9–12: Bring working leg back to *tirebouchon, développé en avant*, and still turning *en dehors*, describe *grand rond de jambe en l'air*, turn to 1st *arabesque*.
Bars 13–14: *Relevé* to *demi-pointe*, pass raised leg through 1st position to 4th position *croisé en avant, demi-plié*, and 2 *pirouettes en dehors en attitude*, finishing *attitude croisé* (supporting leg *fondu*).
Bars 15–16: Drop raised leg into 4th position *croisé en arrière*, 3 *pirouettes en dehors*, continuing into *pas de bourrée renversé en tournant*, finishing 5th position *en face*.
Repeat to opposite side.

2   [Music, slow valse, sequence takes 8 bars] Commence 5th position *en face*.

Bars 1–4: Raise working leg *en avant* to 90°; *relevé* on *demi-pointe*; fall on to raised leg in 4th *en avant*, leaving other leg *pointe dégagé en arrière*. Step backwards on to *demi-pointe*, raising working leg into *tirebouchon en avant*; still on *demi-pointe*, *développé à la seconde* at 90°; *fondu* lowering raised leg into 1st position and immediately *grand battement jeté en avant en tournant*, jumping into 1st *arabesque* (i.e. *arabesque effacé* with supporting leg *fondu*).

Bars 5–8: *Fouetté sauté en tournant* (make one complete turn), raising both arms to 3rd and finish *arabesque fondu à deux bras*. Close 5th position *devant en face*. *Plié* and with a jump *grand battement en arrière*, passing raised leg through 1st to 4th position *croisé en avant*; *Failli effacé* and pass raised leg through 1st to step on *demi-pointe*, raising other leg to *tirebouchon devant*; bend body backwards, raising R arm to 3rd and rounding L arm round waist.

Repeat on opposite side.
(*See illustrations, page 69*).

ALLEGRO

1 [Music, slow mazurka, or 6/8, sequence takes 8 bars] Commence 5th position *en face*.

4 *assemblés doublés (battus) dessous*.
4 ditto   *dessus*.
Repeat twice in all.

2 [Music, 2/4 or march, sequence takes 8 bars] Commence 5th position *en face*.

1 *petit jeté en arrière sur le cou de pied devant*.
1 *sissonne fermée en arrière*.
Repeat 4 times in all.

Reverse movement, i.e.

1 *petit jeté en avant sur le cou de pied derrière.*
1 *sissonne fermée en avant.*
                    Repeat 4 times in all.
            Repeat whole sequence twice in all.

3 [Music, mazurka, beat and open legs on 1st beat and close on
   3rd beat of bar, sequence takes 8 bars]

   Entrechat six, finishing in 2nd position.
   Echappé, closing feet in 5th position.
            Repeat 8 times in all on alternate feet.

4 [Music, grande valse, sequence takes 4 bars] Commence 5th
   position *effacé*.

   Glissade en avant (see note 7, page 65); *cabriole en avant*, pass raised
   leg through *tirebouchon* into 3rd *arabesque* (supporting leg *fondu*);
   pas de bourrée en tournant dessus.
                    Repeat 4 times in all.
                    Repeat to opposite side.

5 [Music, 2/4 or 6/8] Commence 5th position *croisé*, travelling
   diagonally forwards.

   Sous-sous, opening both arms to 2nd and returning to preparatory
   position; turning *en face*, *échappé* (i.e. open and close legs into
   2nd in same jump, and close with opposite foot front.
   Repeat sequence 8 times slowly with *demi-pliés* between each
   jump.
                    Repeat 8 times without *demi-pliés*.
   Then repeat, travelling straight forwards using 1 *pirouette en
   dehors*, finishing 5th position *devant* between the *sous-sous*.
   N.B. The same timing and tempo should be maintained
   throughout both sequences.

6   [Music, valse, sequence takes 8 bars] Commence 5th *effacé*.

Bars 1–4: *Pas de bourrée en arrière* (last step is preparation for) *cabriole battu en avant effacé* (i.e. turning to left); with a half-turn *en dedans* drop into 3rd *arabesque* (i.e. fall on to L *fondu*; *coupé dessous*, raising L into *attitude en avant*.
Bars 5–8: *Relevé en tournant en dehors*, holding L in *attitude*; *pas de bourrée en avant* (i.e. 3 running steps); *grand jeté en avant* into 2nd *arabesque*; immediately change *épaulement* to *effacé* on opposite side and repeat sequence.
> Repeat 4 times in all on alternate feet.

7   [Music, 6/8, sequence takes 2 bars] Commence 5th position *effacé*.

Sissonne battue fermée en avant à deux bras.
Sissonne battue fermée à la seconde dessous, turning *en face* and closing 5th position *derrière*.
Sissonne battue fermée en arrière, raising R arm to 3rd and opening L to 2nd. Hold 5th position.
> Repeat on opposite side.
> Repeat 4 times in all on alternate feet.

8   [Music, 2/4, sequence takes 16 bars] Commence 5th position *en face*.

16 *grand emboités en arrière*, arm in 2nd (i.e. with spring off both feet make one complete turn *en dehors*, raising R *tirebouchon derrière* and closing R 5th *devant* between each turn).
> Repeat to opposite side.

9   [Music, very flowing valse, sequence requires 32 bars] Commence 5th position *écarté sur les pointes* and travel diagonally forwards.

Pas de bourrée courus sur les pointes, changing leading foot and direction every 8 bars. R arm is raised slowly into 3rd when travelling to right, the L is in 2nd.

> Reverse arms when travelling to left.
> Repeat 4 times in all on alternate feet.

10   [Music, quick march, sequence takes 16 bars] Commence 5th *en face*.

Grand battement à la seconde at 90°, bring raised leg *tirebouchon* and bend body towards raised leg. Close 5th *derrière*.
Repeat bringing raised leg to *tirebouchon devant* and bending body slightly away from raised leg, and closing 5th *devant*.

11   [Music, valse, sequence takes 16 bars] Commence 5th position *en face*.

3 *grands battements à la seconde* at 90°, closing working leg 5th *devant*, 5th *derrière* and 5th *devant*, on 4th *grand battement* pass working leg through 1st to *pointe dégagé à la seconde* and close 5th *derrière*.

> Repeat to opposite side.
> Repeat 4 times in all on alternate feet.

12   *Ports de bras.*
Repeat as for Monday's *Ports de bras*, but instead of bending sideways, turn the body as far as possible to the right and then to the left with both arms raised in 3rd position.

Friday

BARRE-WORK

1 Repeat Monday's first exercise.

2 *Pliés* [Music, slow valse]

2 *pliés* each in 1st, 2nd, 5th position *devant* and 5th position *derrière*. Head and arms describing the usual *ports de bras*.

3 *Battements tendus* with *flic-flac* [Music, slow march]

2 slow *battements tendus à la seconde*. (2 beats to each *battement*.)
2 quick ditto. (1 beat to each *battement*.)
Flic-flac en tournant en dehors, finishing 2nd position *pointe tendue*.
Repeat reversing movement, i.e. using *flic-flac en tournant en dedans*.

Repeat sequence 4 times in all.
Repeat to opposite side.

4 *Ronds de jambe à terre* [Music, slow 4/4]

8 slow *ronds de jambe à terre en dehors* (2 beats to each *rond*).
8 quick ditto (1 beat to each *rond*).
1 *rond de jambe à terre en dehors* in *fondu* (*fondu* is held throughout this movement), finish *pointe tendue en avant*; quickly pass working foot through 1st position to *pointe tendue en arrière*, whilst straightening supporting leg and repeat sequence using *ronds de jambe en dedans*.

Repeat to opposite side.

5   *Petits ronds de jambe en l'air* [Music, quick 4/4]

Développé en avant (supporting leg *fondu*); carry leg *à la seconde* at 90°, 2 *petits ronds de jambe en l'air en dehors*. (The supporting leg is straightened as the leg passes to the second.)
Bring raised leg into *tirebouchon*.
Développé en arrière (supporting leg *fondu*); carry leg *à la seconde* at 90°, straightening supporting leg.
2 *petits ronds de jambe en l'air en dedans*.
Bring raised leg into *tirebouchon*.
Repeat 4 times with supporting foot flat and 4 times rising to *demi-pointe*.

Repeat to opposite side.

6   *Adagio* [Music, sarabande or minuet]

Développé en avant, carry leg *à la seconde* at 90°, 1 *petit rond de jambe en l'air en dehors*; pause.
1 *petit rond de jambe en l'air en dehors* and immediately carry leg to *arabesque;* pause.
Reverse movement, commencing from *arabesque* and returning raised leg to 2nd at 90°, 1 *petit rond de jambe en l'air en dedans*; pause, etc.
Repeat sequence twice with supporting foot flat and twice rising to *demi-pointe*.

Repeat to opposite side.

7   *Grands battements* [Music, march]

8 *grands battements en avant*, 8 ditto *à la seconde*, 8 ditto into *arabesque*, 8 ditto *à la seconde*.

Repeat to opposite side.

8   *Battements frappés sur le cou de pied* [Music, galop]

4 *battements frappés à la seconde* (accent is on inward movements).
3 *petits battements sur le cou de pied*, opening working leg to *pointe tendue à la seconde* on fourth beat.
Repeat 4 times with supporting foot flat and 4 times rising to *demi-pointe*.

Repeat to opposite side.

9   Exercise for *entrechats huit* [Music, slow 4/4]

Commence 5th position, open front foot sideways with well-stretched toe, pass through 1st and close 5th *devant*; pass foot through 1st and close 5th *derrière*; pass foot through 1st and close 5th *devant*; pass through 1st and close 5th *derrière*.

Repeat reversing movement.
Repeat to opposite side.

CENTRE PRACTICE

1   [Music, 4/4, sequence requires 32 bars] Commence 5th position *en face*.

2 slow *battements tendus en avant*, 2 *à la seconde*, 2 *en arrière*, and 2 *à la seconde*, closing last of these 5th *derrière*.

Repeat to opposite side.

Repeat this sequence twice in all, then repeat whole sequence using *battements glissés*.

2   [Music, slow 3/4, sequence takes 32 bars for both parts]

Commence 4th position *croisé*, L *pointe dégagé en arrière*.
Anacrusis: Touch L *pointe* on floor.

Bar 1: Step on L *demi-pointe*, changing *épaulement* to *en face* and raising R leg *à la seconde* at 90°.

Bar 2: 2 *petits ronds de jambe en l'air en dehors*.

Bars 3–4: During a third *rond, fondu* and bring R arm into 1st; *relevé* and describe *grand rond de jambe en l'air en dehors*, finishing *fondu* in *attitude croisé* with R arm in 3rd and L in 2nd.

Repeat 4 times in all on alternate feet.

Repeat whole reversing movement, using *petits* and *grands ronds de jambe en dedans* and finishing *attitude en avant*.

3   [Music, 2/4, sequence takes 4 bars] Commence 4th position *croisé*, L *pointe dégagé en arrière*, travelling forwards.

Anacrusis: Touch L *pointe* on floor.

Bar 1: *Coupé dessous* on to L *demi-pointe*, changing *épaulement* to *écarté*.

Bar 2: 3 *battements frappés* (accent on the outwards movement during a *fourth battement frappé, fondu* and hold raised leg *à la seconde* at 90°.

Bars 3–4: 3 *pirouettes enchaînés* (*déboules* or *petits tours*) *en avant*, finishing in 1st *arabesque fondu*.

Repeat 4 times in all.

Repeat to opposite side.

4   [Music, 4/4, sequence takes 4 bars] Commence 4th position *croisé*, moving diagonally forwards.

Bar 1: 3 *relevés* on L foot performing 3 *battements sur le cou de pied* during a fourth *battement*, open R leg and fall into 4th position *croisé* in a *demi-plié*.

Bar 2: *Relevé* on L, opening R *à la seconde* at 90°.

Bar 3: 4 *pirouettes enchaînés* to right, finishing with a fall on to R *fondu*.

Bar 4: *Relevé* on R, changing *épaulement* to *effacé* and opening L *en avant* at 90°; lower L *sur le cou de pied*, changing *épaulement* to *croisé* and repeat sequence.

Repeat 4 times in all.
Repeat to opposite side.

ADAGIO

1 [Music, slow valse, each *développé* takes 2 bars, sequence takes 32 bars] Commence 5th position *croisé*; the whole sequence is performed *sur les pointes*.

8 slow *développés croisé en avant* with R. L arm in 3rd and R in 2nd.
8 slow *développés effacé en arrière*, using L leg, L arm in 3rd, R arm in 2nd.

Repeat to opposite side.

2 [Music, minuet or sarabande, sequence takes 8 bars] Commence 1st position *en face*.

Bar 1: *Plié*, arms in preparatory position.
Bar 2: Rise.
Bar 3: *Développé à la seconde* at 90°, rising to *demi-pointe*.
Bar 4: Fall into 2nd position *demi-plié*.
Bars 5–6: 2 *pirouettes en attitude en dehors*, continuing into 2 *pirouettes en tirebouchon en dehors*.
Bars 7–8: Finish *à la seconde* at 90° with both arms in 3rd and supporting leg *fondu*; pause.

Repeat 4 times in all on alternate feet.

ALLEGRO

1 [Music, 2/4, sequence takes 16 bars] Commence 2nd position *en face.*

8 *sauts à la seconde* using *demi-plié* between each.
8 ditto, *without demi-pliés.*
8 *relevés à la seconde* using *demi-plié* between each.
16 ditto, without *demi-plié.*

2 [Music, 6/8, sequence takes 4 bars, i.e. 2 movements to each bar] Commence 5th position *croisé.*

Assemblé en avant, finishing 5th *croisé* in *demi-plié.*
Assemblé à côté dessus, travelling as far as possible sideways and changing *épaulement.*
　　　　Repeat 8 times in all on alternate feet.

3 [Music, 6/8, sequence takes 4 bars, i.e. 2 movements to each bar] Commence 5th *effacé.*

Jeté en arrière and turning *en face, temps levé* describing 2 *petits ronds de jambe en l'air en dehors.*
　　　　Repeat 8 times on alternate feet.
Repeat reversing movement, i.e. using *jeté en avant* and *temps levé* with 2 *petits ronds de jambe en l'air en dedans.*

4 [Music, easy 3/4, sequence takes 8 bars] Commence 5th position *effacé,* travelling diagonally forwards.

Bars 1–2: 2 *Sissonnes battus fermées en avant à deux bras.*
Bar 3: *Sissonne fermée sur les pointes.*
Bar 4: *Relevé* changing *épaulement* to *croisé* and raising R foot *sur le cou de pied devant.*

Bars 5–8: Close R foot 5th position *devant* and with brief *demi-plié*, 2 *pirouettes en dehors*, finishing 5th position *effacé*.

Repeat 4 times in all.

Repeat to opposite side.

5 [Music, 2/4, sequence takes 8 bars] Commence 5th position *en face*.

3 *entrechats quatre*. 1 *Royale*.

Repeat 8 times in all.

6 [Music, valse, sequence takes 4 bars] Commence 5th position *croisé*, travel diagonally forwards.

Soubresaut; *temps levé*, raising working foot *sur le cou de pied devant*, fall into 4th position *croisé en avant*. *Coupé dessous*; *grand assemblé en avant*, raising L arm to 3rd and opening R to 1st palms face towards each other.

Repeat 4 times in all.

Repeat to opposite side.

7 [Music, 6/8, sequence takes 8 bars, i.e. 2 movements in each bar] Commence 4th position *croisé*, L *pointe dégagé en avant*, gradually travel straight forwards.

Pas marché en avant; *cabriole battu en avant*, turning and falling into 1st *arabesque* (i.e. *effacé* and *fondu*); *coupé dessouse*

Repeat 8 times in all on alternate legs.

8 [Music, 6/8, sequence takes 8 bars] Commence 5th position *effacé*, travel forwards.

Pas de bourrée en arrière; *entrechat huit en tournant* and changing *épaulement* to *effacé* and finishing in 5th *demi-plié*; *relevé* into 1st

arabesque, fall forwards on to raised leg, *petit jeté*, finishing *sur le cou de pied devant*. Repeat sequence to opposite side.
Repeat 4 times in all.

9   [Music, slow valse, sequence takes 8 bars] Commence 5th *effacé*, travel diagonally backwards. (Begin sequence on anacrusis. The rhythm of this *pas de bourrée* is very important, i.e. step on R *demi-pointe*, then L *demi-pointe*, then step on R with good *fondu* to give the necessary impetus for the *cabriole*.)

Pas de bourrée en arrière, cabriole en arrière.
Repeat 8 times in all.

Repeat to opposite side.

10   [Music, easy 2/4, sequence takes 4 bars] Commence 5th position *effacé*. The entire sequence is performed *sur les pointes*.

Raise L into *tirebouchon* and close 5th *devant*; repeat taking L through *tirebouchon* and closing 5th *derrière*;
Repeat closing 5th *devant* and changing *épaulement* during brief pause before repeating sequence with R leg.
Repeat sequence 8 times in all on alternate feet.

11   [Music, 2/4, sequence takes 24 bars] Commence 5th *en face*.

16 slow *entrechats six* using *demi-pliés* between each.
16 quick *petits changements des pieds*.

12   [Music, galop, sequence takes 16 bars] Commence 4th position *écarté*, R *pointe dégagé en avant*.

12 *emboités en tournant* (i.e. *petits jetés*), finishing the musical

phrase with swift *pirouettes enchaînés* (i.e. *petits tours*).
Repeat to opposite side.

13 *Ports de bras*
Repeat as for Thursday's *Ports de bras*.

Saturday

BARRE-WORK

1   Repeat Monday's first exercises.

2   *Pliés* [Music, 4/4]

2 *pliés* in 1st followed by *relevé* and open working leg *à la seconde* at 90° (take 4 beats for 1st *plié*, 2 for second and 2 for *relevé*). Repeat this sequence in 2nd and in 5th *devant* and 5th *derrière*, always opening leg *à la seconde* at 90°.
Repeat to opposite side.

3   *Battements tendus* [Music, 2/4]

1 *battement tendu à côté*, drop heel in 2nd, raise heel and close 5th position *derrière*.
1 ditto, closing working foot *devant*.
4 sets quick *battements en croix* (use *glissé* form).
Repeat to opposite side.

4   *Ronds de jambe à terre* [Music, valse]

8 slow *ronds de jambe à terre en dehors*.
8 quick ditto, closing 5th *derrière*.
Immediately repeat sequence using *ronds de jambe à terre en dedans*.
Repeat to opposite side.
(N.B. During the second half of each sequence the music quickens.)

5 *Adagio. Demi-ronds de jambe* [Music, sarabande]

Bar 1: *Dégagé en avant* at 90°.
Bar 2: *Demi-rond de jambe en l'air en dehors à la seconde* at 90°.
Bar 3: *Double petits ronds de jambe en l'air en dehors.*
Bar 4: *Relevé* (i.e. *demi-pointe*). Close 5th position *devant*.
Repeat 4 times in all.
Repeat to opposite side.
Then repeat sequence reversing movement, i.e. using *rond de jambe en dedans*, etc.

6 *Grands battements en croix* [Music, march]

Take 2 beats to each *battement*, the upward movement coming on beats 1 and 3 of each bar.
Repeat 4 times on each side.

7 *Battements frappés sur le cou de pied* and *soutenus* [Music, 2/4]

Bars 1–2: 4 *battements frappés* (accent is on inward movement).
Bars 3–4: 1 *petit battement sur le cou de pied* (rising to *demi-pointe*, open working leg to *pointe dégagé à la seconde* and lowering heel of supporting foot).
Repeat this movement twice in all.
Bars 9–16: 8 *battements soutenus à côté*, holding working leg outwards when in *fondu*, and closing 5th on *demi-pointe*.
Repeat entire sequence twice in all.
Repeat to opposite side.

CENTRE PRACTICE

1 [Music, easy 4/4] Commence 5th position *en face*.

Bars 1–4: 2 sets slow *battements tendus en croix*, closing in 5th position.

Bars 5–6: 2 sets quick *battements glissés en croix*, closing in 5th position.

Bar 7: *Pas de basque* into 4th position *croisé en avant* (use first two steps only), finishing in *demi-plié*.

Bar 8: 2 *pirouettes en dehors*, finish 5th position *derrière*.

Repeat 4 times in all on alternate feet.

2 [Music, valse] Commence 5th position *en face*.

Bar 1: 1 *battement fondu devant*.

Bar 2: *Relevé*, opening working leg *à la seconde* at 90°.

Bar 3: 2 *petits ronds de jambe en l'air en dehors* (on *demi-pointe*).

Bar 4: Close working foot 5th position *derrière*.

Repeat 4 times in all on alternate feet.

Then repeat sequence using *battement fondu derrière* and closing 5th position *devant* after *petits ronds de jambe en l'air en dedans*.

3 [Music, easy 2/4] Commence 5th position *en face*. Commence on anacrusis.

Relevé on *demi-pointe*, 1 *petit battement sur le cou de pied*, making a $\frac{1}{4}$ turn *en dehors, fondu*. Repeat this short sequence 4 times in all. Having returned *en face*, close working foot 5th *devant* and 1 *battement tendu à côté* to change feet and immediately repeat sequence to opposite side.

Repeat above sequence twice in all.

ADAGIO

1 [Music, slow valse, sarabande or minuet, sequence requires 4 bars] Commence 5th position *effacé sur les demi-pointes*.

Bar 1: Slow *développé en avant.*

Bar 2: Fall into 4th position *effacé,* R leg *fondu* and L *pointe dégagé en arrière,* bend body forwards, raising L arm to 3rd and opening R arm to 2nd.

Bars 3–4: Straighten body and with rise on to L *demi-pointe,* slow *développé en avant,* arms remaining as above and the body bending as far back as possible. On last beat close 5th position *devant.*

Repeat 4 times in all.

Repeat to opposite side.

2   [Music, as above] Commence 5th position *en face.*

Repeat above movement using slow *développé à la seconde* at 90°, falling towards raised leg, raising same arm and bending away from leg in *pointe dégagé.*

Repeat 4 times in all.

Repeat to opposite side.

3   [Music, as above] Commence 5th position *effacé.*

Repeat above movement using slow *développé en arrière,* etc.

Repeat 4 times in all.

Repeat to opposite side.

ALLEGRO

1   [Music, valse, sequence takes 2 bars] Commence 5th position *croisé.*

Bar 1: *Assemblé en avant.*

Bar 2: *Soubresaut en avant.* L arm is raised in 3rd and R in 1st, but both arms are straight with palms of hands turned downwards.

Repeat 8 times in all.

Repeat to opposite side.

Repeat reversing movement (i.e. commence 5th position *effacé* and use *assemblé en arrière*, and *soubresaut en arrière*. The head should be turned towards the back foot during the *assemblé* and turned forwards for the *soubresaut*.

2   [Music, 6/8, sequence takes 2 bars] Commence 5th position *en face*.

Bar 1: *Brisé en avant* (see note 8, page 65), *entrechat quatre*.
Bar 2: *Sissonne ouverte à la seconde* at 90°, *pas de bourrée dessous*.

Repeat to opposite side.

Repeat 4 times in all.

Repeat reversing movement, i.e. using *brisé en arrière*, *entrechat quatre*; *sissonne à la seconde* at 90°, raising front foot, *pas de bourrée dessus*.

3   [Music, galop, sequence should take 16 bars] Commence 4th position *écarté*, R *pointe dégagé en avant*.

Chaînés (*petits tours*, *déboulés*), travelling diagonally forwards *sur les pointes*.

Practise to both sides and finishing in various poses.

4   [Music, valse, whole sequence takes 16 bars] Commence 4th position *croisé* R, *pointe dégagé en avant*.

Bar 1: Step on R, *saut de basque*.
Bar 2: Repeat step and *saut de basque*.
Bar 3: Step sideways on R, *cabriole croisé en avant*, raising L arm into 3rd and opening R into 2nd.
Bar 4: Fall forwards on L, dropping L arm to 1st;
Coupé dessous, raising L into *tirebouchon*.

Repeat sequence to opposite side.
Repeat sequence 4 times in all.

5   [Music, slow 6/8, sequence takes 2 bars] Commence 5th position *croisé*, L foot *devant*.

Bar 1: *Relevé* on R and *développé* L *en avant*, raising R arm into 3rd and L into 2nd; drop forwards on to L foot (*fondu*).
Bar 2: Step on to R *demi-pointe*, making a half-turn *en dehors* into 1st *arabesque* and finishing *croisé* in *fondu*; drop backwards on to L, *glissade en avant*. Repeat sequence to opposite side.
Repeat sequence twice in all.

6   [Music, 6/8, sequence takes 2 bars] Commence 4th position *croisé*, L *pointe dégagé en arrière*.

Bar 1: *Coupé dessous*, raising R *tirebouchon devant*; *grand jeté à côté en face*, raising L arm into 3rd and opening R to 2nd, bend body sideways towards supporting leg as it lands in *fondu*.
Bar 2: *Relevé* on R with *développé à la seconde* at 90°, holding body and arms still; fall sideways on L.
Repeat movement to opposite side.
Repeat sequence twice in all.

7   [Music, 6/8, sequence takes 4 bars] Commence 5th position *en face*.

Bar 1: *Glissade devant*; *relevé*, raising R *sur le cou de pied devant* and changing *épaulement* to *effacé*.
Bar 2: Jump twice *sur les pointes*, holding R leg in *demi-attitude en avant*.
Bar 3: Jump twice *sur les pointes*, describing 2 *ronds de jambe en l'air* with working leg.
Bar 4: With a fifth jump on flat foot change *épaulement* and

carry working leg into *attitude en face, pas de bourrée dessous sur les pointes.*

Repeat sequence 4 times in all.
Repeat to opposite side.

8   [Music, 2/4, sequence takes 16 bars] Commence 5th position *en face.*

Entrechats six, opening legs into 2nd position and with another spring close 5th position *derrière.*

Repeat 8 times in all.

9   [Music, valse, sequence takes 16 bars] Commence 5th position *effacé.*

Bar 1: *Pas courus en avant* (i.e. running steps).
Bar 2: *Grand jeté en attitude croisé.*
Bar 3: *Assemblé en arrière.*
Bar 4: 2 *quick entrechats six.*

Repeat 4 times in all.
Repeat to opposite side.

10   [Music, galop, one sequence takes 16 bars] Commence 5th position *croisé,* travelling diagonally forwards *sur les pointes.*
16 *pas de chat à pointe,* changing feet and *ports de bras* with each step, i.e. jump on R, L foot draws a tiny circle with beat on floor (Russian *flak*), hold R arm in 3rd and L in 2nd. Reverse arms as jump is taken on L, when L arm will move to 3rd and R fall into 2nd.

Repeat twice in all.

11   [Music, 3/4, sequence takes 16 bars] Commence 5th position *croisé.*

16 *grands pas de basque*, legs passing through *tirebouchon* and the arms being raised through 1st to 3rd and opening to 2nd on each *pas*.

12 [Music, valse, sequence takes 4 bars] Commence 4th position *croisé*. L *pointe dégagé en arrière*.

Bar 1: *Assemblé en arrière*, closing 5th position *demi-plié*.
Bar 2: Jump on R, opening L *à la seconde* at 90°, whilst executing double *rond de jambe en l'air en dehors*.
Bar 3: Jump into 2nd position *à terre*.
Bar 4: Jump on to L, passing R through *tirebouchon* to *pointe dégagé croisé en arrière*; repeat to opposite side.
    Repeat 4 times in all on alternate feet.

13 [Music, slow 6/8, sequence takes 2 bars] Commence 5th *écarté*, travelling diagonally forwards.

Bar 1: *Grand pas de chat* to 4th position *croisé*, lifting legs slightly behind body. 3 small *pas de chat* from 4th to 4th.
Bar 2: *Pas de bourrée dessous* changing *épaulement*; raise R leg into *tirebouchon* (*fondu* on L), spring upwards passing R leg behind L in *tirebouchon*, spring upwards again passing R leg in front of L in *tirebouchon*, and close 5th position *devant*.
    Repeat sequence to opposite.
    Repeat whole sequence 4 times in all.

14 [Music, 2/4, sequence takes 16 bars, the accent is upwards on the 1st beat of each bar] Commence 5th position *en face*.

Bar 1: 1 *grand battement à la seconde* at 90°, closing 5th position *derrière*. 1 ditto, using opposite leg.
Bar 2: 1 ditto, finishing by closing working foot through 1st to 4th position *croisé pointe dégagé en arrière*; *fondu* on supporting leg,

gliding working leg further backwards and opening arms to 2nd.
Bars 3–4: *Ports de bras*, i.e. bend forwards lowering arms to
preparatory position and, as body stretches upwards and bends
backwards, raise arms into 3rd; when body returns to upright
position, open arms outwards to 2nd.
Bars 5–8: Repeat *ports de bras*, but more slowly, and close back
foot into 5th position *derrière*.

        Repeat sequence commencing L foot.

15 [Music, slow 4/4, sequence takes 16 bars] Commence 5th
    position *en face*.

Repeat sequence reversing movement, i.e. 2 *grands battements à la
seconde* at 90°, closing working leg 5th position *devant*, at third
grand battement pass working foot through 1st to 4th position
croisé en avant with *pointe dégagé*; keeping weight firmly on back
foot *fondu*, and glide front foot further forwards. Repeat *ports de
bras* as before.

        Repeat sequence to opposite.

16 *Grands changements de pieds.*

TECHNICAL NOTES

1   *Grand rond de jambe en l'air en dehors*

When performed at the beginning of each day's exercises this is peculiar
to the Russian school: Commence 5th position raising working leg into
tirebouchon ouvert (*attitude en avant*), carry the leg without changing its
pose to the side (the leg from thigh to knee should be at least at right
angle to the body, possibly higher), now carry the leg backwards into
attitude. This last position is more open than in the Italian and French
schools; lower the leg to *pointe dégagé en arrière*, pass the foot through
1st position and raise the leg again in front.

Grand rond de jambe en l'air en dedans

Reverse the above movement by raising the leg first into *attitude*, carry
it to the side and then to *attitude en avant*, lower to *pointe dégagé en avant*,
pass it through 1st position and raise again to *attitude*.

   N.B. The leg is raised strongly on the 1st beat of each bar.

2   *The Positions of the Arms*

The positions of the arms are those used in the Vaganova school: i.e.
Preparatory: Both arms curving easily downwards from the shoulder,
the tips of the middle fingers all but touching about a hand's span from
the body. *First:* Both arms raised and curved easily in front of the chest,
tips of middle fingers all but touching. *Second:* Both arms raised and
opened to the side just below shoulder level. *Third:* Both arms raised
and curved above and just in front of the head.

It is important to note that every exercise should start with a *ports de bras*. This can be the arms being raised from preparatory through 1st to 2nd position before the exercise actually begins. At this moment there is always the slightest movement from the wrists and fingers upwards, "The breath of the movement" as it is called. Only after this does the exercise proper commence.

3   Arabesques

The *arabesques* are those of the Vaganova school: i.e.

First: Standing *effacé*, same arm as supporting leg raised in front, the other arm stretched backwards (but never too far behind its own shoulder), the glance is straight forwards.

Second: Standing *effacé*, opposite arm to supporting foot raised in front, the other stretched backwards, the glance is turned to audience (i.e. across shoulder of front arm).

Third: Standing *croisé*, opposite arm to supporting leg in front, other arm stretched backwards, glance is straight forwards.

Fourth: Standing *croisé*, the body now develops a greater curve as the same arm as supporting leg is swept forwards and the other is swept well backwards. The head is turned and inclined towards the audience.

4   All Elevation

All types of jumps, unless otherwise stated, commence with and finish with a strong *demi-plié*.

5   Glissades

The toes never leave the ground in any *glissade*.

6   Glissade en avant

Glissade en avant frequently commences from 4th position, the back foot making the first movement, the second step is then passed through 1st to 4th position, both feet are kept well turned-out.

7   Natural Epaulement

The natural *épaulement* used in movements such as *jetés battements*, *battements tendus*, etc., which travel directly forwards or backwards, are: when travelling *en avant*, the same shoulder comes slightly forwards as the foot coming front and the head turns over that shoulder; when travelling *en arrière*, the same shoulder goes backwards as the foot moves back but the head turns or inclines over the other shoulder.

8   *Brisé en avant* and *Brisé en arrière*

The Russian *brisés en avant* and *brisés en arrière* are equivalent to the *brisé dessus* and *brisé dessous* of other schools, but both movements have a greater degree of travel, the former is taken from *écarté* travelling well forwards, and the latter from *écarté* travelling well backwards. *Brisé volé* is the only other *brisé* so-called in the Russian school. All other *brisés* type steps are classified under some form of *assemblé*.

9   *Tirebouchon*

Tirebouchon is the very high *retiré* position used in the Russian school. The working leg is raised, knee bent so that the tip of the toe rests either in front, at the side, or behind the centre of the knee cap of the supporting leg, whilst that part of the leg from thigh to knee is at least at right angle to the body.

Thursday

Adagio No 2 from Centre Practice

Bars 1—4

Commence 5th en face, *right foot front*

Raise working leg en avant *to 90°*

Relevé

Fall on to raised leg in 4th en avant, *leaving other leg* pointe dégagé en arrière

Step backwards on demi-pointe, *raising working leg into* tirebouchon

Développé à la 2ème

Fondu

Close into 1st position

Immediately grand battement jeté en avant en tournant

Jumping into 1st arabesque, *landing* fondu

Bars 5—8

The following five pages indicate the complete fouetté sauté en tournant *sequence, making one complete turn, raising the arms to 3rd and finishing* arabesque fondu à deux bras

Close 5th position devant en face *and* demi-plié

With a jump, grand battement en arrière

With a jump, grand battement en arrière

Having passed leg through 1st to 4th position, croisé en avant

Failli

Failli

Commencement of coupé *before raising leg in* tirebouchon

Tirebouchon devant

Rise

Raise arm to 3rd and back bend

Raise arm to 3rd and back bend